Both, Apollo

Both, Apollo

Mary G. Wilson

OMNIDAWN PUBLISHING
OAKLAND, CALIFORNIA
2022

Cover Art: Danilo Oliveira, @dnlooliveira

Cover typefaces: Adobe Bernard Modern and Adobe Minion Pro
Interior typefaces: Adobe Cronos Pro and Adobe Minion Pro

Cover and interior design by Ken Keegan

Library of Congress Cataloging-in-Publication Data

Names: Wilson, Mary G., 1983- author.
Title: Both Apollo / Mary G. Wilson.
Description: Oakland, California : Omnidawn Publishing, 2022. | Summary:
"Both Apollo speaks from inside the bodies and binaries that are felt as
constraints. Sometimes it tries to negotiate. It laments, celebrates, reasons,
jokes, and occasionally begs. It runs into a wall and hugs it, offers it pizza, and
speeds through the rotary of grammars and cities until dizziness catapults it
from the grid. It tries to queer the echoes of its language in the hope that a
queer rhyme might break the logic of either/or and give rise to both/and. It
would rather evade than refuse. It would rather embrace than hold. It's basically
a love poem to whatever has the grace to appear. But the battleground is not
all battle, even if there is no safe place above the fray. Moments of humor and
tenderness accompany the speaker with each act of crossing and circling back.
If the poems hope, this is where and how they do it: quietly, at the boundary."—
Provided by publisher.
Identifiers: LCCN 2022007223 | ISBN 9781632431066 (trade paperback)
Subjects: LCGFT: Poetry.
Classification: LCC PS3623.I585555 B68 2022 | DDC 811/.6--dc23/eng/20220217
LC record available at https://lccn.loc.gov/2022007223

Published by Omnidawn Publishing, Oakland, California
www.omnidawn.com   (510) 237-5472
10 9 8 7 6 5 4 3 2 1
ISBN: 978-1-63243-106-6

Across the street there is a house under construction,
abandoned to the rain. Secretly, I shall go to work on it.

—Frank O'Hara

Let's Have Both

That was winter clicking into place.
That was one queer passing
as a boy-child, where the child part
is mostly under-thought. It's strange, when
by the rotary's confusion we eat our lunch
by the public song we get weirdly bored—
though yesterday we had the most ecstatic pizza
under trees—their white-throated rumor
it's always private, but this is just grammar
for what we intuited, isn't it?

A History Of (Dis)Order

At last, the power tools are exhausted.
I wouldn't name them if I owned them
a rough-hewn cabinet of dried bouquets
I'm writing a book called "Surprised by Metal"
whose sentience insults this room—
and then sets fire to the magazine
which isn't mine, and explodes—
I wish you were here.

In general I have either
the whole or the part, never both
the lungs to be extremely lyrical with
to prompt these rocks.
But forgive me—
I got a good deal on this money order
I reaffixed the bird bath with a pie pan
and there it sits,
waiting to get washed.
I adore you. And either my logic is valid
and this world is a duplex.

Taking the dog out to piss
I found myself in a pantheistic landscape
green in praise of the rain we got.
But like grass I have a hard time
seeing the quotidian as a unit of gratitude
which is why my diary is seasonal
and unrehearsed.
And I've stuttered in the face
of a beautiful prose
open at the mouth from which
I could never write it.

These days I'm doing everything therapeutically.
I have an adult coloring book and one black pen.
I'm not optimistic, but I do have hope.
And the smiles that play among Hart Crane's stones.
Do they want me to find them.

This is not my hope:
that if one broken mood
can pause beneath a rope swing
look to the horizon
and take root, there must be creatures
better than ourselves.

This is not my hope:
to find a stranger's diary
on a park bench and share
with their absent body—
their genderless script—
a moment of pure recognition.

This is not my best light either.
Settled in the hole that resembles
gathering strength until I can begin
to go swimming.
And it isn't June yet. My motto of
sleep or be slept in—
could you read it aloud to me?

It Isn't June Yet

I take some space
hold the slim boat's
migration dish across.

Why don't you meet me
on the bench, or don't you
just meet me?

Some feet from.
A calm geology's settled form.

Why would we reason
like a toy if we didn't
on some level
want to break it?

A personhood of streets
a brotherhood of pronouns
spell it out and so
come to what it can't admit.

Creep of fog over
wrinkles the peninsula.
Work brought me to this ____.
I will but it's not mine.

Grain

1.

Former dearest, I am easy to trap
and to explode.
Doves collect the splinters
eagles the doves
photographs the eagles
and the windhover works hard
in a small way
to stay just where it's vibrating—
a twitch in the wing
you know, stirred up.
The butterflies are pornographic.
I dare not look at my phone.
And the sun is a violence today
isn't it—the eclipse really
almost not happening.

2.

When the world was young
I offended you in a poem
in the east-coast summer of the tar fumes
having, with the storm-fast leaves
the hubris to think I could.
And to measure my pulse
this weird contraption
as if the DOI or FDA
spelled us out in corn stalks
holding hands with the other corn.
That's how pastoral it got.
The solar eclipse is less than one
percent at these coordinates.
I forget how it works.
And will spend the day deciding
should I google it later
with the butterflies, who
are so much to be watched
in areal movement.
We—I mean I, dare not check
our phones / my phone.

Bíos / Biós

I love that paragraph
you texted me a picture of
how social the wildlife
in our absence rebounded
In the morning
I take half then wait, then
may be another half
so yes, she is better
I never use windshield wipers
I always throw everything away

Pictionary

Scandals just get better with age.
It's fall and already
the ceiling explodes with new tenants.
Already the capital is wide, pointy and explicit.
And we who have buried our heart in a season
and lost it, like a squirrel with just one nut
wake to a springtime of declined
probabilities. Churn the landscape
with our one tongue, the house
is fire, *try over there.*
Blossoms, cherry and dogwood.
I saw a bird it was great.
The king writes *Nation* with a capital *N*
and why not? We could just start doing that.

Let's Have Both (II)

Between the goddess versions
of Apollo and D-
I am utterly lost.
They pretend to be identical
which is seemly in women
(identical with women)
so of course I'm in love.
But with whom.
They each have a tell but they won't.

It's what our just hearts added
to the general fog material.
Always machinery. Can't they shred
those branches someplace else.
I have eaten my vegetables and for what
rule of threes—
this glimpse of the hill facing east
an animal that won't go to sleep
while in the west, your impossible face.

Hello, you've met my animal
but not myself. Hölderlin
had a word that meant both
war, which is order
and chaos, which is party.
This beach rarely says no, like I do
doesn't it? And out on the horizon
the ocean is pool-colored
unused to being compared with
other than itself.

Like when you accidentally engender
competition by doing stuff.
The fallout is almost a praise poem.

And his beard was frosted with the coldness of years
and thus he spake—

your word-play kindles joy in me
the years abroad, seeking anecdotes
I always say no at the wrong time
since being *for* is not like being *with*

without, withal

Our "nature" excludes the reasonable feel
his reason the rage involved in speeding
towards a red-light, who is god of wine and parties.
It's an old conflict. Why would we catapult
"reason" from this sidewalk if we didn't
want to break it, accidentally
on the hood of someone's car?
And so come to its parts.

When you can't frustrate the logic you started with
or tell a green dress from a great gymnast
or wind from the normal shadows we grew up with
from the bridge where the wind comes in
in spite of geometries over us
and calling out the assholes including their works
and need something to write most vigorously
these days for other people.

This is why our "daily" isn't—
but could be
defined in the box that's an ocean
or staid in the dark
but lovingly gazed on—
a file that writes without stopping
a sparrow running on its little legs
(I think it's a sparrow—
(I think those are legs—

Who declined the wind in their career
early on, because it was myth.

When in doubt, and emerging
sharply into perspective.

Or streaking from one
extreme to the other
in their oh-so-serious
golden carriage.

Last Lyric Donut

I won't bite you about this opinion
that it goes badly with us
professionally—
I'm basically a bachelor
or like   a moment
known as a holiday
for kids.
I can't remember what
that feels like.

I mean, I can
but it's not "like"   anything
enough anymore—
each pink dawn
diving into
the hollow of   this donut
          my doubt—
it's basically the 'O' between eating
and being awake

Manifesto

There's a saying that this battle
evokes procedure, and the glass it metaphored—
and the much we didn't make of it—not
while partying—to follow the procedures
of the violent, and make a cage of this
saying that isn't one.
I carried your name like a huge shield,
a bowl for the apology—
I turned it over and expressed
my disappointment with the soup
which was gross—
the shield sat hold-side down & vacant
liquid seeking out the table's rim—it was
the avant-garde—was green, almost alive
as a weapon—I apologized for
the metaphor and I do—I'm still hungry
is there a word for that

Resume

Once I met a wild boar. She was a rescue.
I mean she is, her name is Fancy.
I wonder if anyone will ever say my name in a poem.
The only god I worship is the one that makes
the future tense conditional, like work experience.
You have to have a job to get a job.
It would be hard to work in.
In Philadelphia the ruin of the Penitentiary
offered more square feet per person
and fewer years per foot
than any current super-max industrial
"facility" with language, but experiment with telling
tour groups that and some of them will hate you
like you just put their shoes on backwards for them.
Time expands some ways.
You know which ones I mean.
Like a haunted house is supposed to be filled
with the ghosts of white bodies.
Like, "don't fuck this up for us."

A Disaster Of Endocrine Proportions, Or, Every Chakra Is Basically Fucked

1.

Wanting to open the door
I opened three.

The third time
it was the right door.

The forum says
a shadow of

a raw nerve
in the weekend

and *sickness*
but loved ones—

this is not my brain

2.

Even the sun
irritates, while sitting

on the waves
by the rocks

I man-spread
not at them

but near them

3.

To the bow   *(Biós)*
he writes

slender of neck
what thrills

for my shade my voice

is given the name
of life (Bíos)

demands emotion of
is not forthcoming

and its work is death

the spore-print of "want"
we meet at the pump of imperatives

lately become excessive
all in hardened

futures and gauze, scoured
metal and word lists

in the not-hope
they'll make wells of you

Inbox

It has a good, sonic flavor. An ending
to hostilities. The blue eye a visual
pun on state secrets, or does it [blink]
rather reveal them?

The city exiles poets in the form of
put them in the audience
somebody has to.
In the language of praise, a toast
can be had, made, or simply toasted.
The news can be read or not, but not
unread. Which is worse for us.
In the longish summer.

In the longish summer
that's how we got by.
Lighthouse to the low
water kayak punting. I'm
pretty sure of it.

The Great Divorce

-After C. S. L.

For the ghosts in paradise
the grass is diamond-hard
and cutting

and the water, though solid
flows out from the place they must go.

For all I doubt the universal
truth this allegory loves,
its landscape so combines
the sense of challenge and
the sense of ease

that I find myself in this
gray town where all is possible
drawn to its uncoupled logic.

Attributions

pg. 23: *I carried your name like a huge shield*
Susan Howe, "Chanting at the Crystal Sea" in *Frame structures,*
Early Poems (1974–1979), pg. 61.

pg. 27: *To the bow (bíos)... is given the name of life (biós)...and its*
work is death
Fragment from Heraclitus, qtd. in Jacques Lacan, *Four*
Fundamental Concepts of Psychoanalysis

Acknowledgements

My warmest thanks to the editors who have published previous versions of the poems included here. "Bíos / Biós" was published in *Elderly* (Number 32), "Let's Have Both," "Let's Have Both II," and "A History of (Dis)order" appear in *Paperbag* (Number 12), "Resume" appears in *Typo* (Issue 31), and "Grain" was published in *The Scores* (Issue 7). Thanks also to the friends and teachers who have engaged with some of these poems along the way: To Lyn and the members of the graduate poetry workshop at the University of California, Berkeley, to Geoffrey, Cecil, Jane, Simona, Eliot, Chantz, and many more, and to Carrie.

Author Bio

Mary G. Wilson is the author of the chapbook *Not Yet* (Projective Industries, 2019). Her poetry has appeared in *Elderly*, *TYPO*, *Paperbag*, *The Scores*, *Coconut*, *Anomalous*, *Macaroni Necklace*, and elsewhere. She holds an MFA from Brown University and a PhD from the University of California, Berkeley. She is from Worcester, Massachusetts.

Both, Apollo
Mary G. Wilson

Cover Art: Danilo Oliveira, @dnlooliveira

Cover typefaces: Adobe Bernard Modern and Adobe Minion Pro
Interior typefaces: Adobe Cronos Pro and Adobe Minion Pro

Cover and interior design by Ken Keegan

Printed in the United States
by Books International, Dulles, Virginia
On 55# Glatfelter B19 Antique 360 ppi
Acid Free Archival Quality Recycled Paper

Publication of this book was made possible in part by gifts from
Katherine & John Gravendyk in honor of Hillary Gravendyk,
Francesca Bell, Mary Mackey, and The New Place Fund

Omnidawn Publishing
Oakland, California
Staff and Volunteers, Spring 2022
Rusty Morrison & Ken Keegan, senior editors & co-publishers
Laura Joakimson, production editor and poetry & fiction editor
Rob Hendricks, editor for *Omniverse* & fiction, & post-pub marketing,
Sharon Zetter, poetry editor & book designer
Liza Flum, poetry editor
Matthew Bowie, poetry editor
Anthony Cody, poetry editor
Jason Bayani, poetry editor
Gail Aronson, fiction editor
Jennifer Metsker, marketing assistant